THE MISSISSIPPI

AMERICA'S GREAT RIVER SYSTEM

MISSISSIPPI

By
Corinne J.
Naden

◄— A FIRST BOOK —►

FRANKLIN WATTS, INC. / NEW YORK / 1974

Map by George Buctel
Cover by Mark Rubin Design

Photographs courtesy of: Chamber of Commerce,
Memphis, Tennessee: 48; Greater Cincinnati Chamber
of Commerce: 7 (upper) ; Greater Minneapolis Chamber of Commerce: 57; Greene Line Steamers, Inc.: 28,
42; Library of Congress: 14, 25 (upper) ; Louisville
Chamber of Commerce: 51; Mississippi River Commission, Corps of Engineers: ii, 3 (upper), 7 (lower),
10, 22, 25 (lower), 33 (upper right), 47; New York
Public Library Picture Collection: 39; St. Louis Re-
gional Commerce and Growth Association: 54; State
Historical Society of Colorado: 19 (upper) ; State
Historical Society of Wisconsin: 3 (lower), 19 (lower) ; Tennessee Valley Authority: 33 (upper left and
lower), 34.

Library of Congress Cataloging in Publication Data

Naden, Corinne J
    The Mississippi; America's great river system.

    (A First book)
    SUMMARY: A history of the longest river system in
the United States, the Mississippi, and a discussion of
its commercial importance today.
    Bibliography: p.
    1. Mississippi River—Juvenile literature. [1. Mis-
sissippi River]   I. Title.
F351.N25   917.7   73-14702
ISBN 0-531-00819-3

CONTENTS

To Harold C. Vaughan, fellow author and friend

A TRIP DOWN THE "GREAT RIVER"

The Mississippi is the longest river system in the United States and one of the major river systems of the world. A *river system* includes the main river and all of its branches, known as *tributaries*. The Mississippi has hundreds of tributaries, adding up to more than 15,000 miles of waterway.

Some people claim that the Mississippi is the longest river in the world. Others say that Egypt's Nile River is longer. It all depends on what figures are used. However, a standard figure given for the length of the Nile is 4,150 miles. According to the Mississippi River Commission, the Mississippi measures 3,986 miles, making the Mississippi the second longest river in the world. It is slightly longer than the Amazon River in South America, said to be 3,900 miles in length.

Measuring the exact length of a major river is a difficult task. The Mississippi, for instance, has many twists and turns along its course. As it meanders down the valley, the river sometimes swells from heavy rains and may create a new loop or bend, adding to its length. Sometimes the waters cut through a bend, shortening its length. The process goes on, year after year.

In terms of *drainage basins* — the land area that drains into a river — the Mississippi comes in third. The Amazon and the Congo in Africa drain greater areas of land. The Mississippi River system drains an area of over 1,243,000 square miles, about one-third of the United States. It receives water from thirty-one states and two provinces in Canada.

The Ojibway Indians of Wisconsin must have been impressed by the Mississippi. They called it *Missi Sipi*, which in their language means "Great River." The river is also known as "Father of Waters."

In one way, however, perhaps the Mississippi River is incorrectly named. The main river is formed by the joining of its three principal tributaries — the Missouri, the upper Mississippi, and the Ohio. Of the three branches, the upper Mississippi is the shortest, some 1,500 miles less in length than the Missouri. The upper Mississippi also has the smallest drainage basin of the three: 171,500 square miles as compared to the Missouri's 530,000 and the Ohio's 202,000. So, in the terms of statistics, it might seem that America's major river system should more correctly be called the Missouri. But the upper Mississippi was the first main branch of the river to be explored by white men, so it has given its name to the entire system. However, the length of this river system is never measured from the *headwaters*, or source (where a river begins), of the upper Mississippi, but always from the headwaters of the Missouri.

Above, the meanders of the Mississippi are clearly shown as the river curves its way through the city of New Orleans. Note ships at anchor in the background. Below, the Missouri appears calm and peaceful as it flows over Rainbow Falls, near Great Falls, Montana.

(2)

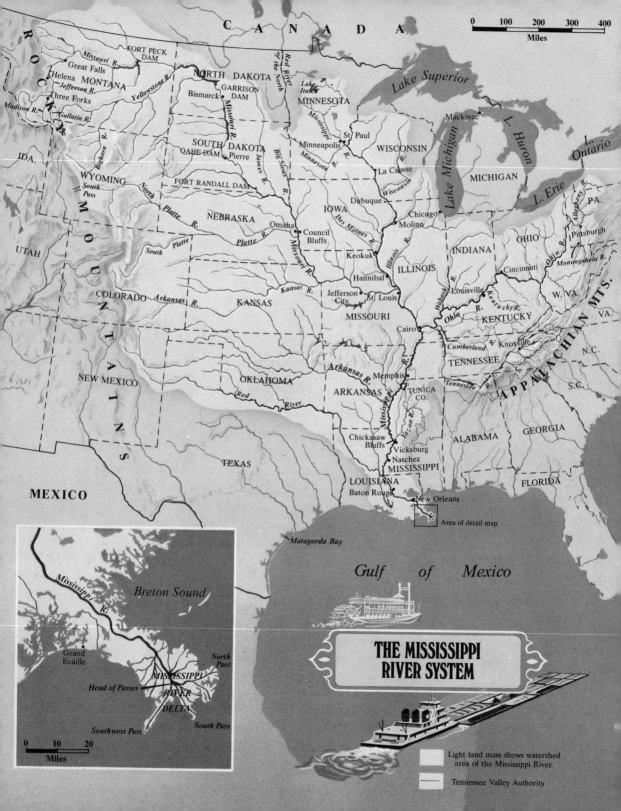

CANADA

ROCKY MOUNTAINS

Madison R.
Missouri R.
Great Falls
Helena MONTANA
Jefferson R.
Three Forks
Gallatin R.
IDA.

FORT PECK DAM

Yellowstone R.

NORTH DAKOTA
Bismarck

GARRISON DAM

Missouri R.

Lake Itasca
MINNESOTA

Mississippi R.

Red River of the North

Lake Superior

Mackinac

L. Huron

WYOMING
South Pass

Bighorn R.

SOUTH DAKOTA
OAHE DAM
Pierre

FORT RANDALL DAM

James R.

Big Sioux R.

Minneapolis
St. Paul

Minnesota R.

WISCONSIN

La Crosse

L. Ontario

UTAH

North Platte R.

South Platte

NEBRASKA
Omaha
Council Bluffs

Platte R.

Des Moines R.

Dubuque

Wisconsin R.

Lake Michigan

MICHIGAN

L. Erie

PA.
Allegheny R.
Pittsburgh
Monongahela R.

COLORADO
Arkansas R.

Kansas R.

KANSAS

Missouri R.

Keokuk

Hannibal

Jefferson City
St. Louis

MISSOURI

Illinois R.

ILLINOIS
Moline

Chicago

INDIANA

OHIO

Ohio R.

Cincinnati

Louisville

Wabash R.

Kentucky R.

W. VA.

NEW MEXICO

OKLAHOMA

Red River

Arkansas R.

ARKANSAS
Memphis

Chickasaw Bluffs
Vicksburg
Natchez

Cairo

KENTUCKY

Cumberland R.

TENNESSEE

Tennessee R.

Knoxville

VA.

N.C.

S.C.

APPALACHIAN MTS.

TEXAS

Mississippi R.

TUNICA CO.

Yazoo R.

MISSISSIPPI

ALABAMA

GEORGIA

MEXICO

LOUISIANA
Baton Rouge

New Orleans

Area of detail map

FLORIDA

Matagorda Bay

Gulf of Mexico

100 200 300 400
Miles

Mississippi R.

Breton Sound

Grand Ecaille

Head of Passes

MISSISSIPPI RIVER DELTA

North Pass

South Pass

Southwest Pass

0 10 20
Miles

THE MISSISSIPPI RIVER SYSTEM

Light land mass shows watershed area of the Mississippi River.

Tennessee Valley Authority

Therefore, the Mississippi River system begins its nearly 4,000-mile journey high in the mountains of western Montana. Fed by mountain springs and melting snows, the Gallatin, Madison, and Jefferson rivers unite near the city of Three Forks to form the mighty Missouri, probably named for a tribe of Sioux Indians.

The longest river in the United States, the Missouri winds its way for some 2,714 miles to join the upper Mississippi a few miles north of St. Louis, Missouri. On its way, beyond Montana's capital city of Helena, the river has cut a deep gorge which is known as "Gate of the Mountains." From there it flows north and northeast through spectacular mountain scenery, past Great Falls, and on across the state to the Fort Peck Dam, largest earth-filled dam in the world — over 200 feet high, two miles long, and half a mile wide. The lake behind it extends upriver for 180 miles. Fort Peck Dam holds enough water to cover the whole state of Montana to a depth of two and a half inches.

All along its twisting route, the waters of the Missouri are swelled by tributaries. One of the larger branches, the silt-filled Yellowstone River, flows across southern Montana to join the Missouri close to the North Dakota border. Turning, then, south and southeast, the widening Missouri flows through North and South Dakota, where the capital cities of Bismarck and Pierre, as well as numerous other towns, have been built along its banks.

Forming the boundary between Iowa and Nebraska, the Missouri travels south to the city of Omaha. On its way it is joined by such streams as the Big Sioux and the larger Platte River. It is said that about 275,000 tons of top soil ride past Omaha on an average day. This soil, continually being washed away into the swirling river water, has given the Missouri its nickname of "Big Muddy." Its yellow waters cause the loss of over 200 million tons of top soil each year. (The entire Mississippi river system carries off about 500 million tons yearly.)

The Missouri is not an easy river to navigate. Its considerable length necessarily carries it through widely changing scenery. It becomes foaming waterfalls in the mountainous areas, broad swirling currents in some parts of the Great Plains, and sometimes only a trickle of water in the arid regions, where dangerous sand bars emerge.

Below Omaha and Council Bluffs, Iowa, the Missouri becomes the boundary line between the states of Missouri, Nebraska, and Kansas. At Kansas City, Missouri, the river turns east on the last lap of its journey to meet the upper Mississippi. As it winds across the state, it is joined by a number of tributaries, including the Kansas River. Flowing past Missouri's capital of Jefferson City, the river snakes its way to a point about seventeen miles above the city of St. Louis. Here, at last, it is met by the upper Mississippi River.

The upper Mississippi in turn, has not been idle. It has traveled 1,215 miles to join the Missouri. The much clearer waters of the Mississippi can be distinguished, flowing side by side with the muddy Missouri, for about 100 miles after the rivers unite.

The Mississippi is born about 1,600 feet above sea level in northwestern Minnesota. Although most maps list its source as Lake Itasca, its true source is probably Elk Lake, five miles above Itasca and about 175 miles south of the Canadian border. Dropping over rapids — at the Falls of St. Anthony, a little north of Minneapolis, the river falls sixty-five feet in less than a mile — and winding through forests, the Mississippi then flows southeast. Below St. Paul, it forms the boundary line between Minnesota and Wisconsin and from this point on, the river remains a boundary between states all the way to central Louisiana.

Above, on its way to join the Mississippi and the Missouri, the Ohio River flows past Cincinnati and its Riverfront Stadium. Below, the Mississippi is relatively narrow here as it passes beneath one of many bridges that span it.

On its journey to meet the Missouri, the Mississippi is fed by a number of important although lesser streams, such as the Wisconsin, the Iowa, and the Illinois rivers. Many, many cities and towns have sprung up along its banks — La Crosse, Wisconsin; Dubuque, Iowa; Moline, Illinois; and Hannibal, Missouri, to name just a few.

About 200 miles south of St. Louis, after having been joined by the mighty Missouri, the river meets its second main branch, the Ohio, at Cairo, Illinois. The blue waters of the Ohio have traveled 981 miles to join the main river. Flowing at a rate of a little more than three miles an hour, the Ohio discharges more water into the conglomerate river system than have either the Missouri or the upper Mississippi. The Ohio has many tributaries of its own; probably the most well-known are the Wabash, the Cumberland, and the Tennessee.

The Ohio River begins in Pittsburgh, Pennsylvania, where the Allegheny and Monongahela rivers come together. From that point, a little over 1,000 feet above sea level, the Ohio travels southwest to join the Mississippi. At Cairo, the river is only a little more than 300 feet above sea level. A number of dams and locks — forty-six in all — help make the Ohio navigable for its entire length — this great river engineering project was completed by the U. S. Army Corps of Engineers in 1929.

Forming the boundary line between West Virginia and Ohio, and then between Kentucky and the states of Ohio, Indiana, and Illinois, the river has influenced the growth of such cities as Cincinnati, Ohio, and Louisville, Kentucky. The name "Ohio" is an Iroquois Indian word meaning "beautiful water." The Iroquois lived around the upper Ohio in the mid-seventeenth century.

From Cairo, Illinois, until its journey's end at the Gulf of Mexico, the great, combined river is known generally as the Lower Mississippi. Although the upper Mississippi has many dams across its waters, there are no dams on the river from Cairo to the Gulf. This is the river of Mark Twain's boyhood, of paddlewheel steamboats, of bustling Memphis, and beautiful New Orleans. The mud-yellow waters of the lower Mississippi twist and turn in a series of loops and horseshoe bends on its 1,000-mile journey to the sea. It flows through a great valley largely of its own making.

The width of the lower Mississippi generally ranges from 800 to 1,500 yards. In some places it widens to about a mile and a half; in others it narrows to about 300 yards. It is a deep river, usually 50 to 100 feet.

About midway between Memphis, Tennessee, and the Louisiana border, the Mississippi is joined by another large tributary, the Arkansas River whose drainage basin — 187,000 square miles — is larger than that of the upper Mississippi. The Red River, which joins the Mississippi in central Louisiana, also has a huge drainage basin — some 93,000 square miles.

Below the Red River, the Mississippi when in flood loses itself in a maze of bayous (by-ooze). These are swampy, sluggish water channels carved in the soft land and formed where a river deposits its silt — fine grains of rock and clay particles.

A little more than 100 miles from its mouth, or end, the Mississippi reaches the port of New Orleans. Here the river is over 100 feet deep, but once past the city it again becomes a maze of twisting bayous and shallow lakes. The land itself is low and flat with the highest points being the levees (great man-made dikes to keep the water back from the land), and they are only 20 feet above the river. Over the past 150 years, the Mississippi has added about 50 square miles to the state of Louisiana as it continually deposits its silt at the delta. This delta area is rich in oil and gas. The deepest oil well in the world — 22,000 feet — is located here at Grand Ecaille, and oil rigs extend out into the Gulf for 30 miles.

The Mississippi River officially ends at Head of Passes. It is to

this point that its length is counted. Actually, however, it travels about 20 more miles to the sea through five main channels. The two most widely used by ships are South and Southwest passes. With frequent dredging, they are kept to a depth of about 35 feet.

Once free of the channels, the Mississippi's long journey brings it at last to the Gulf of Mexico.

Building or repairing levees, or dikes, to
hold back the river water is a never-ending task.

DISCOVERING THE MISSISSIPPI

The first white man to see the Mississippi River was a Spanish explorer named Hernando de Soto (about 1500–1542). To him, this major river of North America was just another barrier in his search for gold.

Spain had already found rich gold and silver deposits in South America. Near the mid-sixteenth century, explorers began to look to the north for these precious metals. De Soto landed in Florida in June, 1539. That winter he and some 700 men began the march north in search of great wealth. For four years De Soto explored what are now the states of Georgia, South and North Carolina, Tennessee, and northern Alabama and Mississippi. But there was no gold or silver to be found.

From the beginning De Soto and his men suffered great hardships. Many died of cold and starvation; many were killed in Indian attacks. The Spaniards in turn slaughtered many Indians in their march through the wilderness.

De Soto reached the Mississippi River on May 8, 1541. He called it the Rio Grande, "great river" in Spanish. With about half of his men alive, he crossed the wide, muddy river, still in search of treasure.

There remains some dispute today over the spot where De Soto first crossed the Mississippi. Citizens of Tennessee say the event took place at Chickasaw Bluffs, south of Memphis. Mississippians disagree, pointing out a site in Tunica County, about forty miles below Chickasaw Bluffs.

After another year of fruitless search in what now are the states of Texas and Arkansas, De Soto returned to the Mississippi. But he had caught a fever (probably malaria) and soon died. Fearful of Indian attack, his men buried him in the river, telling the Indians that De Soto was a god and his body had gone to the sky.

In March, 1543, the survivors of De Soto's expedition built boats, sailed down the river to the Gulf, and reached the coast of Mexico, which was a Spanish colony.

For over a century, the river was just a name on the inaccurate maps of the New World. Then, on June 17, 1673, two French explorers discovered the upper Mississippi. Father Jacques Marquette (1637–1675), a Jesuit missionary, and explorer Louis Joliet (1645–1700) set out to find the great river reported by Indians in the area. They wanted to know if the river led south to the Gulf of Mexico or southwest to the Gulf of California (between Sonora, Mexico, and Baja California).

From the northern shore of Lake Michigan, the two men and their Indian guides traveled over 600 miles before reaching the river. Marquette grandly named it *Rivière de la Conception* (literally translated as "river of conception"), but it continued to be called by the simpler Indian name of *Missi Sipi.*

Marquette and Joliet continued their exploration of the Mississippi as far south as the mouth of the Arkansas River. In doing so,

they saw the mouths of both the great Missouri and the Ohio rivers.

Around the time of Marquette and Joliet, another Frenchman began to explore the Mississippi. His name would become one of the most famous to be linked with the river. Had the dream of René-Robert Cavelier, Sieur de la Salle, been realized, the history of the United States might have taken a far different course.

La Salle (1643–1687) was born in Rouen, France, and sailed to New France in 1666. New France was the name given to French possessions in North America, mainly that area which is now Quebec Province in Canada. He became interested in exploring the territory after joining a group of missionaries who set out in 1669 to convert the Indians to Christianity.

After parting with the missionaries, La Salle began a search for the river that the Iroquois called the Ohio. Some historians credit him with discovering the river in 1670, but more recent research does not support that theory. La Salle himself did not claim discovery of the Ohio River.

By the time La Salle returned to New France, he had a great vision in mind for his native land. From his talks with Indian tribes, he had become convinced that the Mississippi River flowed all the way to the Gulf of Mexico or possibly even to the Pacific Ocean. His vision was to claim all that area for France. He would build a French Empire in the New World, a vast territory with the Mississippi River as its natural waterway. Had he succeeded, the heartland of North America — from Quebec to the Gulf and west of the Mississippi to the Rockies — would have become a French colony.

Certainly La Salle did not fail for lack of trying. In 1677 he asked the French government to grant him twenty-year control over all the lands he might explore and develop. But the government was afraid that too much expansion might weaken French resistance

Early fur trappers and Indians engage in battle on the Missouri River.

against the English and Dutch in the area around New France, so it granted him only five years.

Disappointed but not discouraged, La Salle began his great expedition in 1678. For the next two years he traveled from Fort Frontenac (present Kingston, Ontario) to the Illinois River. Attacked by hostile Indians and traders, often half frozen and starving, he nevertheless managed to set up a chain of French forts along his route.

But La Salle knew that the chain was stretched too thin. In order to strengthen it, he spent most of 1681 talking to Indian tribes in the area. He wanted them to join the French in a great federation.

By December of that year La Salle had rallied the support of a number of tribes, as well as the government of New France, for an expedition which would go from the Great Lakes to the Gulf. Traveling down the Mississippi River, past the Missouri, the Ohio, the Arkansas, he claimed territory after territory for France. The Indians on the land were often pleased by La Salle's friendliness but generally were unaware that he was, in fact, taking their lands.

In April, 1682, with the Gulf of Mexico before him, the young Frenchman solemnly claimed for his king all the land he had explored. He had proved that a great north-south waterway did, indeed, exist in the New World.

Unfortunately for La Salle, and for France, not everyone regarded him as a hero. Upon his return to New France, he found the government now controlled by men who seemed intent upon discrediting him. So La Salle sailed to France in 1683 to see the king. There he discovered that his government now wished to establish a French settlement on the Mississippi delta as a threat to the Spanish. La Salle agreed to head the project.

The explorer's last adventure began in July, 1684, when he sailed from France, planning to land at the mouth of the Mississippi. He reached the Gulf coast in December, but he was lost. Not having any idea where the river was, he decided to go ashore and continue the search on foot. It was a tragic decision.

La Salle and his expedition landed at what is now called Matagorda Bay on the southeastern Texas coast, about a three-week walk from the Mississippi. Time and again he tried to find the river, but he could not. Finally, the Frenchman and twenty of his party set out in early January, 1687, on yet another search for the river. In March the dream of the young explorer was ended. The long search had taken its toll of his men. Sick and starving, some of them turned against him and one of them shot him in the head. The plan for a new French Empire had failed.

On the 1678 expedition La Salle had been joined by a young Italian soldier named Henry de Tonti. As second in command, Tonti had been left in charge of the Illinois forts. In 1689 he sailed down the Mississippi, hoping to find any survivors of the colony La Salle was to build in the delta. The search was a failure, but during the next few years Tonti made many trips up and down the Mississippi and he added much to the growing knowledge about the great river. When Tonti died in 1704, the Mississippi, from north to south, was charted on fairly accurate maps.

Two other men are given credit for spreading knowledge about the Mississippi and encouraging settlers to the area. One was a Belgian missionary named Louis Hennepin; the other an American army captain, Jonathan Carver.

Hennepin (about 1640–1701) had come to New France in 1675 and joined La Salle's expedition three years later. In 1680 he was sent to explore the area of the upper Mississippi. Captured by Sioux Indians near present-day Minneapolis, he was released a year later. Hennepin went to France in 1682 and published two books about his travels — *Description de la Louisiane* (Description of Louisiana) in 1683 and *Nouvelle Découverte d'un Trés Grand Pays Situé dans l' Amerique* (New Discovery of a Very Large Land Located in America) in 1698. These two accounts were widely read, despite the fact that Hennepin was less than truthful in them, at least about some of his own accomplishments. He claimed to have been the first European to have seen the mouth of the Mississippi, which he was not.

Jonathan Carver (1710–1780) also wrote about the Mississippi. Born in Massachusetts, Carver taught himself mapmaking. In 1766 the governor of the British post of Michilimackinac (now Mackinac in Michigan) asked Carver to map the rivers in Minnesota and Wisconsin. As a result of this expedition, Carver wrote a book called *Travels in Interior Parts of America* (1778). His description of the upper Mississippi valley was so glowing and readable that many settlers came to the area.

Although a good deal was known about America's major river by this time, no one knew its source, or where the Mississippi began. That knowledge did not come until the nineteenth century. In 1805 President Thomas Jefferson sent Zebulon M. Pike to look for the headwaters of the Mississippi. An army lieutenant who would later discover the peak named for him in Colorado, Pike traveled into present-day Minnesota, less than 100 miles from the river's source. It was not until twenty-six years later that geologist Henry Rowe Schoolcraft discovered Lake Itasca and proclaimed it the source of the Mississippi. (Today the true source is believed to be Elk Lake, which empties into Itasca.)

Above, an early French map to the Louisiana Territory. Had the explorer La Salle been successful, the heartland of North America would have become a French colony. Below, while charting the Missouri, Clark and his men stop to shoot bear. Their 1804-06 expedition opened the American northwest to settlers and trade.

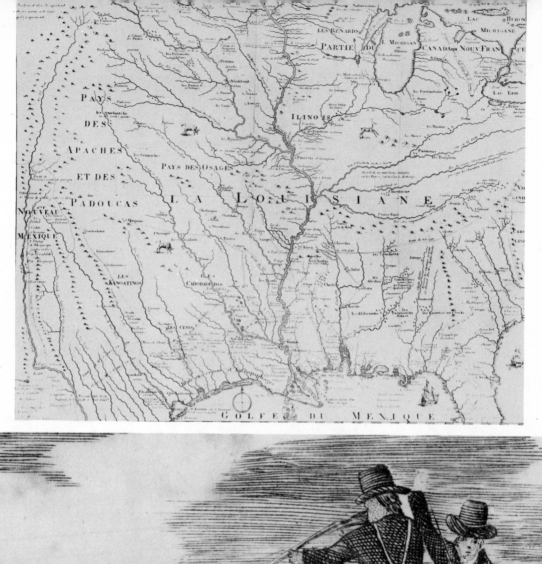

During all the time that details were being gathered about the Mississippi, exploration was progressing slowly on its major branch, the Missouri. French trappers were probably the first white men to see this longest American river, and the first to explore and chart it was probably a French explorer, Etienne Veniard de Bourgmond, who followed the Missouri about as far as the Platte River in Nebraska around 1714.

The Missouri remained largely the territory of the French during much of the eighteenth century. In 1803 France sold the co-called Louisiana Territory, about 885,000 square miles west of the Mississippi and including the Missouri basin, to the United States for 15 million dollars.

Father Marquette had charted the mouth of the Missouri in 1673. In 1803 President Jefferson sent explorers Meriwether Lewis and William Clark to chart the Louisiana Territory, including the Missouri. During their 1804–06 expedition, Lewis and Clark traveled the Missouri to its source in Montana, then went on to the Snake River, which led them to the Columbia and the Pacific Ocean. They returned down the Missouri, reaching St. Louis in September, 1806.

Lewis and Clark opened the Missouri basin to settlers. Five years after their expedition, a trading post had been opened near the mouth of the Columbia River.

Although other explorers would travel the mighty Mississippi and its branches, charting the great river system more accurately each time, the river had already become a highway of commerce by the 1820's. In ever increasing numbers barges and steamers plied its waters between New Orleans and the Ohio River. The upper Mississippi was opened to traffic in 1823. The river's importance to the economic life and growth of the United States had begun.

THE RIVER AT WORK

It would be difficult to make too much of the Mississippi's importance to the growth of the United States. It is the nation's largest natural waterway. Before the white man came to the New World, Indians paddled the waters of the Mississippi. In the early and growing years of the country, the river and its tributaries were the major means of transportation. At that time people and materials simply could not have moved from place to place as quickly and as easily as they did had it not been for the Mississippi River. New Orleans became a major world port largely because of the Mississippi. American cities grew and prospered because of their locations on the main river and its branches. The raw materials for industries and finished products for sale at home and abroad all reached their destinations by way of the Mississippi.

Today people and goods travel about the country in many ways. The steamboat as a vital part of American economic life is gone, and with it is gone a great deal of the passenger traffic on the river. Yet,

the Mississippi, especially in the South, is still an important water highway, and New Orleans remains a major port.

Up until the nineteenth century, the Mississippi was mainly important as a means for explorers and settlers to reach different parts of the country. Its development as an avenue of commerce began in the early 1800's when steamers and barges began to crowd the river with raw materials and manufactured goods.

The first steamboat to travel down the Mississippi arrived in New Orleans on January 12, 1812, with a cargo of cotton. (Sugar was the first successful money crop on the river, but cotton soon replaced it.) The steamer was owned by the Ohio Steamboat Navigation Company, with inventor Robert Fulton, Robert R. Livingston (who negotiated the Louisiana Purchase as minister to France in 1803), and Nicholas J. Roosevelt (President Theodore Roosevelt's great granduncle) as partners. The first trip took three and one-half months, starting from Pittsburgh.

Two years later Captain Henry M. Shreve built the steamboat *Enterprise* and also sailed from Pittsburgh to New Orleans. Then he went back upriver to Louisville, proving that river traffic was profitable both ways.

By 1814 twenty-one steamboats docked in New Orleans. Five years later there were 191 arrivals, by 1833 the number had reached 1,200, and by 1840 New Orleans was the fourth busiest port in the world. After 1823, when the first steamer (*Virginia*) reached present-day Minneapolis, the entire length of the river was open for business.

The great paddlewheelers churned through the Mississippi waters at six miles an hour going upstream and ten miles going down. They carried immigrants from Europe and cotton for Europe, traders

Industries, as well as cities and towns, prosper to a large extent because of their locations on the river. This is a lumber company in Vicksburg, Mississippi.

and settlers, products for the developing West, travelers to St. Louis and points north.

Traffic on the Mississippi continued to increase, reaching its height shortly before the Civil War, at which point commerce was disrupted by the hostilities.

The Mississippi played an important role in this war. The South had some forts along the lower river, but did not arm the river towns. Apparently, the Confederacy did not see what the Union did — the importance of being able to use the Mississippi to transport men and supplies. By controlling the river, the North would also divide the southern states.

Thanks to the Union navy, the Mississippi had become a Union river by 1863. Many southern forts were captured in early 1862. The city of Memphis surrendered in April, after the Union navy destroyed the Confederate gunboats anchored there. New Orleans was captured. So were Vicksburg, Baton Rouge, and Natchez. The Mississippi belonged to the North, and that fact helped the Union to gain victory over the South.

After the Civil War, the rapid growth of the railroad systems across the United States gradually reduced commerce on the Mississippi. However, in 1917 during World War I, it boomed again. Because the railroads were struggling to meet war demands, the government created the Federal Barge Lines and pressed all available river craft into service to carry war supplies.

After the war, the Transportation Act of 1920 kept the government in business on the river and provided for the start of improve-

Above, the Union naval fleet patrols the river during the Civil War. Union control of the Mississippi aided the north in its victory. Below, "pushing" barges down the lower Mississippi. Barge traffic is slow, but it is also profitable because many barges can be handled together.

ments to the river channel. By 1937 the Army Engineers had largely completed the huge system of dams and locks which make the Mississippi navigable. Dams between St. Paul and St. Louis really turned the Mississippi into a series of navigable lakes. The river channel was deepened to nine feet throughout.

Keeping the Mississippi opened for traffic is a never-ending task. The channel depth must be constantly checked, a job performed by survey boats. Dams and dikes must be kept in excellent condition. Between St. Louis and St. Paul are some 800 brass, oil-burning channel lights. The lights are white and hang on twelve-foot-high posts. They are refilled every three days by people living along the river, who are paid a certain amount to keep the lights burning.

Today the Mississippi moves a lot of freight on barges. Sugar, oil, coffee, and rice travel north; flour, lumber, and threshing machines go south. Gravel, steel, stone, soybeans, sulphur, and many, many other products are shipped on Mississippi barges.

Although barge traffic is slow (a barge is towed at about six miles an hour), many barges can be towed together, and they carry cargo at about half the rate of the railroads. Each barge can carry between 500 and 1,500 tons of cargo, about the capacity of an entire freight train. Barges on the river are not actually towed; they are pushed because it is easier to handle a barge when it is being pushed. Modern towboats use Diesel engines, and have sophisticated electronic gear for navigation and communication.

Commerce on the Mississippi and its tributaries continues to grow. Twenty-five million tons of cargo were shipped in 1920, and the figure reached over 100 million by 1945. In the ten-year period between 1962 and 1971, the total number of tons of traffic on the river system increased from over 257 million tons to nearly 400 million tons. Using 1971 as a sample, crude petroleum was the leading cargo on the Mississippi, with over 21 million tons shipped that year. Corn was second, soybeans third, and aluminum ores fourth. The 1971 leading cargo for freight traffic on the river was gasoline, followed by crude petroleum, coal and lignite, and corn. The river's busiest port by far is New Orleans, with a total of over 120 million tons of shipping in 1971, followed by Baton Rouge (more than 47 million tons), and St. Louis (about 11 million). In 1971 passenger and dry cargo ships made over 9,000 trips up and down the Mississippi; tankers nearly 3,000; tugboats close to 1,500; and barges 1,600. About one and a half million people were passengers.

So the Mississippi remains a busy water highway, in a twentieth-century manner. Yet, there is still at least one place on the river where it is possible to recapture the past. One riverboat which carries passengers overnight still sails the Mississippi. Called the *Delta Queen*, it is operated by Greene Line Steamers of Cincinnati, Ohio.

Built in 1926, the *Delta Queen* is a carefully preserved antique paddlewheel steamboat. It has a steel hull and a wooden superstructure. It is licensed by the Interstate Commerce Commission and regularly inspected by the United States Coast Guard. Because of its partly wooden construction (which cannot be changed and still preserve the ship), the *Delta Queen* does not meet the requirements of the 1966 Safety at Sea Law. Designed to protect American citizens from unsafe foreign ships on sea voyages, the law also included the paddlewheeler. The *Delta Queen* does contain fire detection and automatic sprinkler systems, and has fire retardant coatings on most overheads (ceilings) and bulkheads (walls). After historic-minded citizens called for an exemption, Congress, in August, 1973, excluded the steamboat from the 1966 law for at least five more years.

Passengers can take trips of varying lengths from several different ports. The *Delta Queen* operates from February to the end of October. A voyage from Cincinnati to New Orleans, one way, takes seven steamboat days, and can cost from $210 to $350. The passage includes room, meals, and entertainment.

This lovely white paddlewheeler has two 1,000-horsepower steam engines which turn the giant (28-foot) red sternwheel. Its 75 officers and crew make about 50 journeys each season, touching more than 100 river towns and sailing through 17 states. It is a trip straight from the nineteenth century, with everything kept as authentic as possible. And just as they did a century ago when the steamboat came into view, small children along the banks of the Mississippi can be heard to shout "Steamboat's comin'!"

Above, they're not "waiting for the Robert E. Lee," *but for the* Delta Queen, *a carefully preserved antique paddlewheel steamboat, the only remaining overnight passenger riverboat on the Mississippi.*

FLOODS AND FLOOD CONTROL

From ancient times to the present day, floods have been one of man's great enemies. They are responsible for thousands of deaths and millions of dollars in property damage. They ruin the land; they destroy crops; they waste water.

One of the earliest known floods occurred in China in 2357 B.C. Floods have been recorded in North America as early as 1543, when a member of De Soto's party wrote of a flood on the Mississippi. Ever since, the Mississippi and its branches have been the cause of most of the flood destruction in the United States. Marquette and Joliet witnessed a flood on the Missouri in 1673. The Ohio River flooded a number of times during the eighteenth century, as did the Mississippi in the nineteenth. In 1903 a great flood in the Mississippi and Missouri river basins caused the deaths of 100 people and damages of over 40 million dollars. Enough water poured into the Ohio River from its branches in a 1937 flood to have covered the state to a height of four feet. In 1951 the Kansas River flowed over Kansas City, leaving behind a billion dollars worth of destruction.

Today the loss through flood damage in the United States ranges between $200 and $500 million yearly. These figures are recorded by the National Weather Service and the U. S. Army Corps of Engineers, which keep flood statistics for the nation as a whole. The Ohio River basin (from Pittsburgh, Pennsylvania, to Cairo, Illinois) suffers from more flood damage than any other area. Largely because of the flood control system begun after a disastrous 1927 flood, the lower Mississippi accounts for only about seven per cent of the nation's yearly flood damage.

In the north, floods are usually caused by melting snows. Prolonged rains or sudden intense storms are other causes of flooding. The Mississippi reaches its annual peak (top) flood stage from February to June, and the Ohio from January to April. The Missouri has two peak stages — March and April, after the snow melts in the plains; and June, after the snow melts in the Montana mountains.

There have always been floods, and man has always been trying to control them. The steps taken to keep flood damage as low as possible are known as *flood control*. In the United States, flood control began on a national level when the Mississippi River Commission was established in 1879. Since that time other commissions have been set up, and Congress has passed laws in the continuing effort to control flood damage.

The River and Harbor Acts of 1917, 1927, and 1930 extended national flood control outside of the Mississippi basin. In the Flood Control Act of 1936, Congress set up a national policy of flood control. It recognized two main objectives: regulating the flow of rivers, which is the responsibility of the U. S. Army Corps of Engineers; and preventing soil erosion and reducing water runoff over the land, the concern of the Department of Agriculture. These and other acts are created or amended through the years as we learn better methods to fight flooding.

Flood control measures on the Mississippi and its tributaries stem from an act of 1928. With its amendments, the act is respon-

(31)

sible for actions taken which prevented major flood damage on a number of occasions through the years. Some $850 million has already been spent on Mississippi flood control.

There are four main ways of controlling floods. They are the improvement of river channels; reservoirs; emergency channels; and a system of levees, or dikes.

River channels can be improved by straightening them, widening them, or deepening them to contain more water when necessary. But this method is limited. A channel can be straightened, widened, or deepened only so far or so much.

Flood-control reservoirs are built to hold excess river water for a time. The first reservoirs strictly for this purpose — on the Mississippi and Ohio rivers — were built in 1913. Dammed water can be stored in them to great depths. When the river waters reach a critical stage, the gates, usually located near the base of the dam, are closed, and water begins to collect in the reservoir. When the critical stage is passed, the gates are opened. The most effective and easy-to-build reservoirs are those at the site of a natural lake.

Emergency channels built to hold excess water are an old idea in flood control. However, their feasibility depends on the surrounding land. The flat lands of the lower Mississippi are a good example of an area in which these channels can be effective. They are built by constructing a pair of levees across flat land and, when necessary, excess river water is diverted into them.

Levees, or dikes — probably the most widely used method of flood control — are embankments along the river channel. Their pur-

Above left, flood damage in the United States runs between $200 and $500 million yearly. Here the river waters cover the streets of a city. Right, one way to control floods is by improving the river channel. Below, the Chickamauga Dam on the Tennessee River has a reservoir with a storage capacity of 347,000 acre-feet.

pose is to keep the water in the channel and off the land. Although this is generally a very effective flood control method, a dike system can sometimes make things worse. If the water does get over or break through the levee, it usually does so very suddenly, and people may be caught in the rushing waters.

Depending on the specific location and problem, one of these methods may be used alone or one or more may be used in combination.

The most famous example of the attempt to develop a river basin and control its water is the story of the Tennessee Valley Authority (TVA). It is a federal agency created in 1933.

The Tennessee River, a major tributary of the Ohio, begins just north of Knoxville, Tennessee, and flows for 652 miles southward into Alabama and then north to Kentucky until it joins the Ohio near the southern tip of Illinois. Fifth largest river in the United States in terms of the amount of water flowing in its channel, the Tennessee drains an area that includes seven states — Kentucky, Mississippi, Alabama, Georgia, North Carolina, Virginia, and Tennessee.

Before TVA, the Tennessee basin was subject to periodic floods. Navigating the middle region of the river was nearly impossible due to obstructions. The soil in the basin was worn out, and the region was desperately poor.

These two photographs were taken from Lookout Mountain overlooking Chattanooga, Tennessee. The photo on the left shows Chattanooga during the flood of March, 1867. The photo on the right was taken a century later, in 1967. Dams on the Tennessee River have held floods to minor levels in this area.

Fontana Dam is TVA's highest — 480 feet on the Little Tennessee River in North Carolina. It is the highest concrete dam east of the Rockies.

(35)

In 1933 the Tennessee Valley Authority Act was created, with three aims in mind for developing the river — navigation, hydro-electric power, and flood control. It also sought, through such additional measures as reforestation and soil conservation, to develop a better economic life for the people living in the river basin. Although TVA has not been entirely successful in improving economic conditions, it is a world-famous model of what can be accomplished in developing a river.

Thirty-three major dams on the Tennessee and its branches now regulate the waters. Together they can store over 23,000,000 acre-feet of water. Since their completion no major floods have occurred in the valley. That alone has saved the area millions of dollars in flood damage. The lakes created by the dams are connected by locks, making the Tennessee navigable for just about its entire length.

TVA has been most successful in generating electric power on the Tennessee. This huge power system gives the region the lowest cost for electricity in the country. In other spheres, TVA has created recreational boating and fishing sites, promoted programs of mosquito control and conservation practices, and it has helped to reforest over one million acres of land.

Certainly flood control measures on the Mississippi River system helped to keep down the damages caused by the spring flood of 1973. The flood was said to be the third worst of the century, the result of day after day of spring rain, following a winter of high rainfall. When the ground could absorb no more moisture, the river and its branches began to rise. Seven Mississippi valley states suffered damages amounting to over $200 million, with over 30,000 people left homeless and more than 30 dead. Yet, despite this severe destruction, the dams, levees, and spillways on many parts of the river helped to save other thousands of lives and homes.

MARK TWAIN ON THE MISSISSIPPI

Rivers have always held a special fascination for man. Quite apart from their commercial importance, rivers have a certain mystery and romance, a sense of adventure about them. Say the words "Mississippi River," and they usually bring to mind the romantic steamboat era of the 1800's, when the great paddlewheelers carried passengers and cargo on a 1,200-mile, four-day journey between St. Louis and New Orleans. The Mississippi also brings to mind the name of one of America's greatest writers. Once a river boat pilot himself, his writings captured for all time the picturesque life of a more leisurely, bygone day on the mighty river.

He was born Samuel Langhorne Clemens, but he wrote under many (and often odd-sounding) pen names — W. Epaminondas Adrastus Blab, Petroleum V. Nasby, and Quintus Curtius Snodgrass among them. However, the world knows him best by his most famous — and certainly more simple — pen name of Mark Twain. Although the other names may have come from pure imagination, the name of

Mark Twain comes directly from the Mississippi. First used by Clemens in 1863, the name is really an old river call indicating a water depth of two fathoms, or twelve feet. When the river pilot heard that call, "Mark Twain!" he knew he was in safe water.

Among the most famous of Mark Twain's many works are *The Adventures of Tom Sawyer* (1876), *Life on the Mississippi* (1883), and *The Adventures of Huckleberry Finn* (1884). *Tom Sawyer* (Twain's first novel) concerned a young boy growing up in a small town on the banks of the Mississippi. *Life on the Mississippi* grew out of a series of articles Twain had written about his experiences when he, himself, worked on riverboats. *Huckleberry Finn* tells of the adventures of Tom Sawyer's "bad-boy" friend.

In these three books, and others as well, Mark Twain was writing about a subject he knew well. Like Tom and Huck, he, too, grew to manhood on the banks of the Mississippi River.

Born on November 30, 1835, in Florida, Missouri, Samuel Clemens was the sixth child of John Marshall and Jane Lampton Clemens. The family moved to Hannibal, Missouri, on the shores of what Twain would later call "The great Mississippi, the majestic, magnificent Mississippi" when he was four years old.

Almost at once the young boy was enchanted with the daily arrival of the boat bringing mail and supplies from New Orleans. He never forgot the excitement and romance of watching the boats being unloaded, of "glamorous" people, such as gamblers and minstrel-show actors, stepping ashore into the small Missouri port. And as he dreamed away his summer hours on the river's shores, he vowed that one day he would lead the adventurous life of a steamboat pilot on the Mississippi River.

However, a number of years were to pass before the boyhood dream would come true. His father died in 1847, when Sam was

Mark Twain in later years.

(38)

twelve, and the boy left school to help support the family. The following year he became an apprentice to a newspaperman and was, in a sense, launched on his real career. He rose from typesetter to assistant editor before going to work for his older brother, Orion, who had started a paper, the *Hannibal Daily Journal*. His writings were simple and sometimes childish, but Samuel Clemens had already begun to show the humor and an understanding of human behavior which would become so evident in this later works.

In 1853, when Samuel Clemens was nearly eighteen, he decided to seek his fortune elsewhere. So, after promising his mother he would not drink liquor or play cards (neither promise was kept), he set out for St. Louis on a Mississippi riverboat. For the next two years he worked on newspapers in St. Louis and Philadelphia, and for a book-printing company in New York City. Sensitive and intelligent but lacking confidence in himself, the young man finally gave in to homesickness and returned to his family. By this time he had grown to his adult height of five feet ten inches. He had a strong face, greenish eyes, and auburn hair.

The Clemens family was now living in Iowa. Once again Sam went to work for his brother, who had bought a book and job-printing shop in Keokuk. That job lasted for over a year, until the urge to travel once again overcame him.

During the next few months Samuel Clemens sent back letters of his travels to the Keokuk *Saturday Post*. Printed at $5.00 a letter, they were the first of many to be signed with the young traveler's unusual pen names. The letters were filled with humor and an uncanny grasp of American regional speech differences.

In April, 1857, now 21 years old, Samuel Clemens boarded the riverboat *Paul Jones*, headed for New Orleans. He had decided to go to Brazil, where it was said a fortune could be made from cocoa. Instead, the trip launched his long-wished-for career as a riverboat pilot.

The nineteenth-century Mississippi River steamboat, also known as a packet, was a colorful sight to behold. Its wood-burning furnaces made steam which turned the huge paddlewheels on each side of the boat. The hull was painted white and gaily decorated, usually with red or blue trim. Two smokestacks, with metal strips stretched between them, poured smoke from the furnaces into the sky. The packet's name stood out plainly and proudly on the semi-circular covering over each paddlewheel.

Inside the packet, the bottom deck housed cargo and steerage passengers. Above that were elegant rooms for first-class passengers and also a huge dining room. An orchestra or minstrel show was the usual entertainment. On the top deck stood the window-walled pilothouse. In all this splendor, the riverboat passenger could sail from Pittsburgh to New Orleans for just eight dollars.

Being a riverboat pilot was no easy job. There were no navigational charts of the Mississippi, but they would not have been of much help anyway. The Mississippi is a turning, twisting river, with a high water level today, a low one tomorrow. A sandbar can rise almost overnight, or the river alter its course after a heavy rain. A pilot simply had to know the river, and all the signs of its changing condition, and know it well. People's lives and the safety of valuable cargo depended upon his skill and memory. In spite of careful pilots, there were many accidents. Between 1840-50, for instance, 4,000 people were killed or injured in steamboat accidents.

It took Samuel Clemens eighteen months to know the Mississippi. When he had reached New Orleans aboard the *Paul Jones*, he had discovered that no ships were scheduled to leave for Brazil for some time. With that in mind, he had persuaded Horace Bixby, pilot of the *Paul Jones*, to take him on as an apprentice. Under Bixby's excellent guidance, Clemens was granted his pilot's license in September, 1858.

Pilot Clemens remained on the river until 1861 and the beginning of the Civil War, which closed the Mississippi to commercial traffic. During that time he piloted many different packets, including

The City of Memphis, largest of them all. Most of that time he earned $250 a month. He always referred to those years as among his happiest, and would later put his piloting adventures on paper.

Samuel Clemens had no fierce loyalty to either side in the Civil War and no liking for war in general. So, in the midst of it, he set off to make his fortune in the West. In 1862 he joined the *Daily Territorial Enterprise* in Virginia City, Nevada. A year later he first signed his articles as Mark Twain.

By 1864 Twain had moved again — this time to San Francisco and the *Morning Call,* where he became a reporter. The following year he heard the story of a miner who owned a frog that could out-jump any competitor in any contest. The story became "The Celebrated Jumping Frog of Calaveras County," and it made the name of Mark Twain famous. It was published by the New York *Saturday Press.*

The jumping frog changed the life of Mark Twain. He began to give public lectures and to travel. And he kept writing. In 1869, after a European trip, he wrote *The Innocents Abroad.* His books were published at fairly regular intervals after that. His life changed in other ways, too. In 1870 he married Olivia Langdon and settled down in Buffalo, New York, and then Hartford, Connecticut.

Mark Twain wrote a number of now-famous books during his lifetime. His name became linked with American humor and with the Mississippi River. He spent much time abroad on lecture tours, such as a year-long, round-the-world tour beginning in 1895. In 1907 Oxford University in England granted him an honorary degree of Doctor of Literature. Three years later, on April 21, Mark Twain died of a heart ailment.

The inside of the pilothouse on the
Delta Queen *duplicates the interiors of the*
paddlewheelers in Mark Twain's time.

Perhaps no piece of writing so well illustrates Twain's feeling for his boyhood on the Mississippi as does *The Adventures of Tom Sawyer*. For in a sense, young Tom was actually young Samuel Clemens, a rebel and a dreamer. It is a celebration of the glories and fears of youth, of a more leisurely age long passed, a time to sit on the banks of the wide Mississippi River and dream a thousand dreams.

NEW ORLEANS AND POINTS NORTH

A trip up the Mississippi, starting at the nation's second major port, will take you to some of the most important cities in the United States. All of them were founded, and all of them prospered, largely because of the river.

NEW ORLEANS, LOUISIANA

The port of New Orleans, founded in 1718, was named for Philippe II, duc d'Orléans and regent of France at the time (until Louis XV came of age). Located on about 199 square miles of land, with the Mississippi on its southern border and Lake Pontchartrain to the north, New Orleans is 110 miles upriver from the Gulf of Mexico and a major world trade site. Its economic life centers around the shipping and petroleum industries, although agriculture, manufacturing, and tourism are important, too. The tourist trade contributes over 160 million dollars a year to the city. Many of the tourists come to the French Quarter at Mardi Gras time. The French Quarter is the original part of New Orleans, an area of charming, well-preserved old homes, and streets with names such as Clio, Socrates, and Tchoupitoulas, which latter — perhaps not surprisingly — everyone seems to pronounce in a different way. Bourbon Street is the French Quarter's entertainment avenue. At Mardi Gras time, ending at midnight before Lent, the streets overflow with parading masked dancers.

New Orleans was named the French colonial capital of the Louisiana Territory in 1722, and became part of the United States in 1803 when the Territory was purchased from France. Descendants of first settlers called themselves creoles, to indicate Spanish or French blood.

The last battle in the War of 1812 was fought in New Orleans, when Andrew Jackson defeated the British forces. Linked with the war and with the city is the name of the famous pirate Jean Lafitte.

There were many pirates operating along the lower Mississippi during the late eighteenth and early nineteenth centuries. Lafitte, who had come to New Orleans from France around 1806, was among the most successful. By 1813 there was a $750 price on his head. The following year Lafitte was offered 30,000 pounds in gold by the British (as well as a commission in the Royal Navy) to join forces with them in attacking New Orleans. Lafitte refused. Instead, he offered himself and his men to the Americans. Although affronted at first by such a suggestion from a pirate, Andrew Jackson, a practical man, wisely decided to accept the help he knew he needed. And Lafitte and his pirates did help to save the city. As a reward, President James Madison pardoned all pirates who had joined in the battle. Pardoned or not, Lafitte was snubbed by the military. Eventually, he left New Orleans and sailed away on a new pirate adventure.

The Mississippi flows past the famous French Quarter in New Orleans. Jackson Square and St. Louis Cathedral can be seen in the center of the photograph.

(46)

New Orleans became the main commercial center in the South during the 1800's, largely due to its location. Yet, for many years that same location also hindered its growth. The city is built on swampy land. Lack of adequate drainage became a major problem, and New Orleans at one time suffered through severe yellow fever epidemics; today, pumping stations have solved the drainage problem. The river also brought disaster to New Orleans in time of flood; now the levees along the banks of the Mississippi protect the city from this danger.

Famous for its carnivals at Mardi Gras time, New Orleans is also famous for its superb restaurants and for its music. It is known as the birthplace of jazz. Louis Armstrong heads a list of well-known musicians from New Orleans. Thousands of tourists each year visit the jazz museum in the French Quarter.

Education and sports are an important part of living in New Orleans. It has a number of universities, including Tulane (site of the Sugar Bowl), Loyola, and a branch of Louisiana State University. In the 1960's the city gained a professional football team, known as the New Orleans Saints. (They were named after one of the most famous of all jazz tunes — "When the Saints Go Marching In.")

The temperature in New Orleans averages a little above 70 degrees, and the rainfall is high — more than 53 inches yearly. The city's population numbers over one-half million.

MEMPHIS, TENNESSEE

Located in the southwestern tip of the state, the city of Memphis, spreading out over some 217 square miles, is one of the largest inland river ports in the United States. At high water, the city sits about forty feet above the Mississippi. Three bridges cross the river into the

The Memphis city skyline from the river.

(49)

neighboring state of Arkansas. Memphis is the largest city in Tennessee and the most important center of commerce between New Orleans and St. Louis, Missouri.

Once the home of the Chickasaw Indians, the site became a French fort in 1698 and a Spanish fort about 100 years later. After the Louisiana Purchase, Andrew Jackson was among those who established the first permanent settlement at Memphis in 1819. Seven years later it became a town, with a population of 500.

Today Memphis has a population of more than 623,000. A great railroad terminal, it is also the world's largest hardwood lumber center. The city boasts one of the most well-known streets in the country — Beale Street, a famous name in the world of blues music. W. C. Handy, the great American composer and musician, once lived on Beale Street. His most famous work is "St. Louis Blues," which he composed in 1914.

LOUISVILLE, KENTUCKY

Kentucky's largest city (population over 360,000) lies on the southern shore of the Ohio River, a fact that makes it a great manufacturing center and a major transportation link between ports on the Atlantic and St. Louis. Named for Louis XVI of France, the city was founded in 1778 by explorer George Rogers Clark. Then in the state of Virginia, Louisville grew to a population of about 600 by the end of the century. (Kentucky was granted statehood in 1792.) The arrival of the steamboat brought Louisville to a golden age.

McAlpine Locks and Dam at Louisville. Built in 1960, the lock accommodates the largest river tows. It fills and empties in eight minutes, and can lift or lower river traffic 37 feet. In the lock is the excursion sternwheeler, Belle of Louisville.

Today Louisville is the world's largest tobacco manufacturing center. It also contains automobile plants, a huge appliance manufacturing industry, and is a major producer of bourbon whiskey. But probably its best known product is the Louisville Slugger, long a favorite baseball bat with professionals and amateurs.

Once a year Louisville becomes the most famous city in the sports world. It is the site of the Kentucky Derby, held at Churchill Downs on the first Saturday of May. Over 100,000 fans crowd the racetrack to see the "run for the roses," held annually since 1875.

Louisville owes its growth to the Ohio River, but for many years the river also caused great destruction with its floods — an especially bad one occurred in 1937. However, flood control projects, including a 17-mile-long levee built in 1956, have largely controlled the flood danger in the city and surrounding areas.

CINCINNATI, OHIO

About 110 miles upriver from Louisville is the city of Cincinnati, founded in 1788. It was first called Losantiville, but the name was changed in 1790. By 1795 Cincinnati had 10 houses, 94 cabins, and 500 people.

Today the city has considerably more of everything, including a population of over 450,000. It spreads back from the Ohio for some 72 square miles, most of it hilly land. It is a great transportation link and inland port.

Cincinnati also owes its growth in large part to the Ohio River. As settlers traveled west, they stopped at the settlement and many of them stayed. With the coming of the steamboat, river traffic increased and Cincinnati prospered until the mid 1800's, when the railroads brought about a sharp decline in river traffic. The river also brought great flood destruction to the city, although the completion of canals on the Ohio has reduced that danger today.

Besides being home to the University of Cincinnati, founded in 1819, the city also houses the football Bengals, the baseball Reds, and the basketball Royals. It is a leading producer of machine tools, soap, jet engines, pianos, leather goods, and chemicals.

ST. LOUIS, MISSOURI

On the Mississippi once more, we find the city of St. Louis, known as the "Gateway to the West." It became a French trading post in 1764 and was named in honor of the French king. Fur trader Pierre Laclède picked out an ideal location just below the point where the Missouri meets the Mississippi. Today the stainless steel Gateway Arch stands near the site Laclède had chosen. Designed by the famed architect Eero Saarinen, it is 630 feet high, the tallest monument in the United States.

The city's location has always played an important part in its history and growth. St. Louis became part of the United States with the Louisiana Purchase in 1803. For nearly the first half of the nineteenth century, it was the center of fur trade on the Mississippi. Until the 1850's, steamboat traffic made St. Louis one of the country's main commercial centers. When the railroad replaced the steamboat, the city became a main connecting point between east and west.

Today St. Louis is still a great commercial center, with a population of about 622,000. Besides being a major inland port, it is one of the largest trucking centers in the country. It boasts the world's largest brewery (Anheuser-Busch) and two of the largest American shoe manufacturers. It is the home of both a professional football and baseball team, each called the St. Louis Cardinals. One of its outstanding tourist attractions features trophies of Charles Lindbergh, who made the world's first trans-Atlantic solo flight in 1927 in his plane, The Spirit of St. Louis. The flight was sponsored by businessmen in the city.

(53)

Situated on the west bank of the Mississippi, the city is surrounded by, but not part of, St. Louis County. Eight bridges span the river. The oldest, Eads Bridge, was opened in 1874 and considered an engineering miracle at the time.

St. Louis has four major universities — branches of the University of Missouri and Southern Illinois University, and Washington and St. Louis universities.

KANSAS CITY, MISSOURI

About 235 miles west of St. Louis is Kansas City, located at the junction of the Kansas and Missouri rivers. Its site led to its growth as a main transportation and trade center. It was first explored by French trappers and later by Americans. Daniel Boone's son is said to have been the first American to explore (around 1800) what is now Kansas City. The settlement was known as Kansas Town around 1846 and by its present name after 1889.

Kansas City early became an important market for the agricultural products of the Middle West, and it remains so today. The Hannibal Bridge, the first over the Missouri, was opened in 1869. The city became a major grain and cattle center in the late 1800's. Today, with a population of over 500,000, Kansas City is a leader in the cattle and wheat markets. Meat packing and flour milling are important industries, as is automobile and truck assembly. The city is also a major banking center.

Many colleges and universities, including the University of Missouri at Kansas City, are located here. Kansas City is also home for the Royals (baseball) and the Chiefs (football).

*The landmark of
St. Louis—Gateway Arch—
overlooks the Mississippi.*

Just across the state line is Kansas City, Kansas, which is included in the metropolitan area of Kansas City, Missouri.

OMAHA, NEBRASKA

North-northwest of Kansas City, on the west bank of the Missouri, is Omaha, Nebraska. Largest city in the state, it has a population of nearly 350,000.

Omaha has always been a transportation center, and is, in fact, often called the "Crossroads of the Nation." Named after an Indian tribe, it was first explored by Lewis and Clark in 1804 and became an Indian trading post in 1825. In 1846 Mormons stopped at the site on their way to Utah and built a settlement. First known as Winter Quarters and then Florence, the present city was laid out in 1854 and chartered in 1857.

Today Omaha is a trucking and rail center and has five barge lines which serve the city. It is a livestock market and meatpacking center, as well as a major grain market. Omaha is also the headquarters of more than thirty insurance companies, including Mutual of Omaha, largest accident and health insurer in the world.

MINNEAPOLIS—ST. PAUL, MINNESOTA

On the Mississippi again and far to the north of St. Louis are the so-called Twin Cities of Minneapolis and St. Paul. Together their metropolitan area has a population of close to two million. St. Paul is the smaller of the two; its population is some 310,000 as compared to 434,000 for Minneapolis. Largest city in the state, Minneapolis is located on the Falls of St. Anthony on the Mississippi River and joins St. Paul on the southeast.

The upper Mississippi winds through the University of Minnesota campus in Minneapolis.

Father Louis Hennepin saw the Falls of St. Anthony in 1680, and Jonathan Carver explored the area around the Twin Cities in 1766. The city that became St. Paul was first called Pig's Eye, after one of its original settlers, who for some unknown reason answered to that name. In 1849 it became a town, with a population of over 800. Named capital of the Minnesota Territory, St. Paul remained the capital when Minnesota became a state in 1858. Minneapolis was settled in the mid-1800's and grew into a great flour milling center. It was incorporated as a town in 1872.

Today the Twin Cities remain important manufacturing centers. Minneapolis is still the site of a large milling industry. St. Paul has seven major barge lines, a huge trucking industry, and is a leader in the refining of petroleum products.

The Twin Cities have a number of colleges and universities, including the University of Minnesota. Suburban Bloomington is the home of the baseball Minnesota Twins and the football Minnesota Vikings.

GLOSSARY

Bayous — swampy water channels formed where a river deposits silt.

Drainage basin — land area that drains into a river.

Emergency channel — man-made bed for river water, built to hold excess water in time of flood.

Flood control — steps taken to keep flood damage as low as possible.

Headwaters — where a river begins.

Levees — also known as dikes, man-made walls to hold back river water.

Mark twain — old river call indicating water depth of two fathoms, or 12 feet.

Mouth — end of a river.

Paddlewheeler — steamboat on the Mississippi and its branches.

Reservoir — lake created by dam on a river.

River channel — bed in which river water flows.

River system — main river and its branches.

Silt — rock and clay particles deposited by a river.

Tennessee Valley Authority (TVA) — federal agency created in 1933 to develop the Tennessee River basin and control its water.

Tributaries — branches of a river.

COMPARING THE MISSISSIPPI

Facts about the Mississippi River
and other rivers of the world.

Name	Location	Source	Mouth	Approx. length in miles
Amazon	So. Amer.	Peruvian Andes	Atlantic Ocean	3,900
Colorado	U.S.A.	Rocky Mts.	Gulf of Calif.	1,400
Columbia	Canada	Canadian Rockies	Pacific Ocean	1,200
Congo	Africa	Lake Tanganyika	Atlantic Ocean	2,900
Danube	Europe	Black Forest, Germany	Black Sea	1,750
Ganges	India	Himalayas	Bay of Bengal	1,540
Hudson	U.S.A.	Adirondack Mts.	New York Bay	315
Hwang Ho	China	Chinghai Province	Yellow Sea	2,700

Jordan	Asia	Anti-Lebanon Mts.	Dead Sea	200
Loire	France	Mont Gerbier de Jone	Bay of Biscay	625
Mississippi	U.S.A.	Elk Lake, Minn.	Gulf of Mexico	1,215
Missouri	U.S.A.	Jefferson, Madison, Gallatin rivers, Mont.	joins Mississippi	2,714
Niger	Africa	Fouta Djallon Mts.	Atlantic Ocean	2,600
Nile	Africa	Kagera River (via Lake Victoria)	Mediterranean Sea	4,150
Oder	Europe	Oder Mts.	Baltic Sea	563
Ohio	U.S.A.	Allegheny, Monongahela rivers, Penn.	joins Mississippi	981
Ottawa	Canada	Grand Lake Victoria	St. Lawrence	696
Paraná	So. Amer.	Brazil	Río de la Plata	2,050
Platte	U.S.A.	No. & So. Platte rivers	joins Missouri	310
Po	Italy	Italian Alps	Adriatic Sea	405
Potomac	U.S.A.	Cumberland, Md.	Chesapeake Bay	285
Rio Grande	U.S.A.	San Juan Mts.	Gulf of Mexico	1,800
St. Lawrence	No. Amer.	Lake Ontario	Gulf of St. Lawrence	1,900
Seine	France	Plateau of Langres	English Channel	482
Tennessee	U.S.A.	Holston, French Broad rivers	Ohio River	652
Thames	England	Gloucester	North Sea	210
Tigris/ Euphrates	Asia	Turkey	Persian Gulf	1,150
Volga	U.S.S.R.	Ural Mts.	Caspian Sea	1,570
Yangtze	China	Tibet	East China Sea	3,430
Yukon	No. Amer.	Yukon Territory	Bering Sea	1,800
Zambezi	Africa	Angola	Indian Ocean	1,600

BOOKS FOR FURTHER READING

Anyone who enjoyed this book on the Mississippi River may be interested in the following books on related subjects:

Andrist, Ralph K. and Mitchell, C. Bradford. *Steamboats on the Mississippi*. New York: Harper, 1962.

Eaton, Jeanette. *America's Own Mark Twain*. New York: Morrow, 1958.

Meredith, Robert and Smith, E. Brooks. *Exploring the Great River*. Boston: Little Brown, 1969.

Naden, Corinne J. *The First Book of Rivers*. New York: Watts, 1967.

Proudfit, Isabel. *River-Boy*. New York: Messner, 1940.

Renick, Marion. *Ohio*. New York: Coward, 1969.

Stearns, Monroe. *Mark Twain*. New York: Watts, 1965.

Twain, Mark. *Life on the Mississippi, The Adventures of Tom Sawyer,* and *The Adventures of Huckleberry Finn* in various editions.

INDEX

River systems, 1, 2
Roosevelt, Nicholas J., 23

St. Louis, 6, 8, 20, 24, 26, 27, 53, 55
Sand bars, 6
Schoolcraft, Henry Rowe, 18
Shreve, Henry M., 23
Silt, 5, 9
Snake River, 20
Source of Mississippi and branches.
  See Headwaters.
Steamboats, 9, 20, 21, 23, 24, 27, 29,
  52, 53. *See also* Mark Twain.

Tennessee River, 8, 25, 36

Tennessee Valley Authority, 35,
  36
Tonti, Henry de, 17
Top soil, loss of, 5
Transportation Act of 1920, 24
Trappers, 20, 55
Tributaries, 1, 2

Virginia, 23

Wabash River, 8
War of 1812, 46
Width of Mississippi, 9

Yellowstone River, 5

ABOUT THE AUTHOR

Corinne J. Naden is a graduate of New York University and lives in Fort Lee, New Jersey, on the bank of the Hudson River. She spent four years in the United States Navy (WAVES), where she edited a weekly newspaper and wrote naval training films, and is now a children's book editor in New York City. The author has written several books for children, among them *The First Book of Rivers, The Nile River, Woodlands Around the World, and Grasslands Around the World.*